CONFESSIONS *of a* BELIEVER

DANNY SUTHERLAND

ISBN 978-1-0980-5319-2 (paperback)
ISBN 978-1-0980-5320-8 (digital)

Christian Faith Publishing, Inc.
832 Park Avenue
Meadville, PA 16335
www.christianfaithpublishing.com

Printed in the United States of America

True Sight Unveiled

Time, steady and so elusive
Making the mistake of thinking you have abundance
Betrays you when it runs out
Caught in a bubble
Operating in the here and now
Not knowing that on the next level is a release
That transcends the box we appear to be in
Insight and wisdom can only crack open this enclosure
Revelation that is only God given
The few gifted, viewing so much more than the natural
Carefully ushered into an abundance
That can overwhelm the unprepared
This gift is there for the taking
A byproduct of seeking after the One who made you
God, the ultimate source for an answer
To elusive for mere mortal intellect
The Holy One
The Most High
Jehovah God

Hurt Unreleased

Second chances, other glances
Too proud for conversation
Closed to opportunities
Remembering and feeling wounds
Past hurts so dark
It overshadows a black hole
Wearing a frown
Made from the breaking down of faith
Once alive and flowing
Will it ever change?
(The hurt from long ago)
Feeling like it was just yesterday
Regretting the steps taken
That caused your heart to be an open book
So profound was the love lost
Taking apart and pulling pieces of your soul
Leaving behind an apprehensive and timid shadow
Pieces picked up that are the byproduct of the disaster
Doing and feeling fine
Shows the outward
The inward full of enigmas and lagging pain
Trying to recall a life that was tainted
Through a foggy lens of time

Out of focus
Thinking it was the good life
But in actuality it was killing you softly
Breaking down pillars of marble into a sea of sand
Closing off all opportunities of present fulfillment
Trying to cut off a possible hurt
Before it can occur
Seeking refuge in a life of solitude
Building walls of protection
Until there is no way in or out
Trapped by the very thing built to protect

Personal Gratitude

Jesus I have to tell you
Something that's been on my mind
I know you know the answer
Because you control eternity and time
Now this one thing
You did not have to do
This one thing
Before I had a beginning
Not just for me
You did this for everyone
I thank you dying for me
Way way back on Calvary
Such a love without a price
Your grace is enough for me
I just want to say thank you Lord
For paying the price for me
In everything, God you are good
Perfect, strong, and mighty
You are worthy of all the honor
Your majesty reigns forever
It is time that we give you all the praise
I magnify Your Holy Name
I worship you in spirit and in truth
Hallelujah, Hallelujah, Hallelujah

My Craft

Amped higher than a NASCAR race
Listen closely as I set this pace
So fast miles past without a second guess
Wind blowing through my fingers
As I get a grip
To slippery to hold to accurate to control
My mind an abstract painting
Hard to figure, but always an attention grabber
Pulling words together in a soup
Creating a masterpiece
Hanging them in plain view
Like a web
Capturing the small and big
For a feast, they won't likely to forget
Hanging on the edge of disaster
As my mind moves faster than a speeding thought
Reconciling past unlocked treasures
Stirring and stirring my brew of epiphanies
It becomes clear to me
That once I start I have to finish
Only to begin again from where I leave off
A cycle not so vicious
But ambitious to go beyond this man's limitations
Pushing the cause of one from many

Thinking that my craft will be forever remembered
If I only forget the presence of possible failure
And the absents of not taking that first step
So many snapshots to choose from
How could it ever get boring?
Pulling and sorting from life's rich bounty
A sea of subjects just waiting to be tapped
Storing them in the vault accessing at will
Speaking clearly of one's own view
Limited only by the steady pace of consistent growth
Leaps and bounds I grow hopping into the next phase
Growing into a champion as I weald my gift
Will it get better than this?
Hopefully yes
A long way from the best I claim to be
With humble reservation
I will get their
I'll just keep on writing
Till that one perfect piece
Which always eludes me
Comes to satisfy this ever growing appetite

The Explanation of Me

To understand me is to understand the very nature of an enigma
To try to tear down a puzzle that is not fitted together with the wrong
    instructions
I am a work of art
A masterpiece not made by conventional means
A significant piece of engineering that is of the highest
To know me is to know my story
To know my story you must put away stereotypical philosophies
Breaking down strongholds to expose truth,
you might not be ready for
You must first get a grip and grow up
Easy to say but beyond must capabilities
This might be in words to deep for everyday interpretation but well
    worth the excavation
I'll tell you this
It is or was like the unraveling of consciousness to unconsciousness
    and back
In and out like a prairie dog, on the lookout from its predator
Only it was not as visible as a common enemy
A foe so elusive that punches and round houses
Could not disable it
The answer was a power so great
That even in a hurricane, tornado, and explosion simultaneously

He can be heard in a still small voice
He is so evident and clear
But the masses chose not to acknowledge Him
Though He wants them to
This enemy who Jesus defeated
Used his worst arsenal on me
But was defused like the sizzle of bacon
With little effort and an infant's ease
God saved me to tell my story and this is the beginning

Uncertainty

Uncertainty clothes me like an uncomfortable suite two sizes too small
It disregards my feelings as if it had a silver spoon born in its mouth
It taunts me day in and day out
Pushing and fighting my every effort
What would Jesus do is my constant thought
For God has not given us the spirit of fear
A mighty verse that is in my mind
To take my uncertainty and toss it like a rag doll is my goal
A fight that a lot of times go untold
Trying to wreck my potential and destroy my future before my eyes open
I press toward the mark of the one who called me
Scratching and kicking with every step
I see light at the end of a long dark tunnel
And the dark I have over come
Since I was very young
No choice I had, but to step up and become
Not a hard man, but a wise one
In time I have learned
Opposition is not always negative
Even though it feels like it
It teaches as a byproduct and feeds growth inadvertently
So I look back and see where I thought I was miles back
I have not come as far as I need to be
But I am further than I would be, without uncertainty

Perfect Love

Your perfect love has given me peace
Your perfect love no one else could show or give
Your perfect love brought me through the trials
Your perfect love, your perfect love
I love you, Lord, for you are my shining star
More beautiful than rivers and mountains
More precious than rubies or diamonds
There is no one like you
Now that my eyes are open
I see your Heavenly Glory
Why did I try it alone?
It was a struggle that caused my heart to moan
Before I knew you cared
Before I knew you were there
I struggled with the weight of despair
But now whenever morning comes
I rejoice because that's one more day
That I can live in Jesus name
I bless your name

Shine Your Light

I'll shine Your Light for You
You gave me the strength to survive
And I'll praise Your Name forever more
For you are worthy to be praised
Glory and Honor to Your Name
I want to bless You, Lord
Your Precious Name should be adored
I magnify Your Name
It is because of you that I have survived
Thru the depths and through the heights
You have been my shining light
So, Lord, I need you
Please don't ever leave my side
Because, Lord, You are so beautiful
And I can't help but to lift you up
I love you so much
That's why I'll shine Your Light for You

Tears of Joy

I can't hide the tears of joy inside
Because you have given me more than the world could ever give
You have blessed me with an inner peace
That conquers the enemy's snares
I just want to praise you, Lord
I just want to praise you
You heard me when I cried out to you
You gave me refuge in the time of my storm
You carried me all the way
There are times when the road seems dark and cold
But I know you are there to make a way
I just want to let you know that I love you
And give you the highest praise
Hallelujah to Your Name
How can we say that we love you?
When everything is put above you
But I can only account for me
Striving for that day that I'll be set free
Running towards that time
When all the hard and rough roads traveled
Will be well rewarded
That's why I say thank you, Lord
I know you still care

And there is a place called glory
Reserved for all who serve Him
It was there when time began
It will be there when time ends
If you will only except Him
He will bless you
Take away your heavy burdens
And fulfill your wants and prayers
That's right He is the Lord and He cares
So it's time to give Jesus all the glory
Spreading peace by telling His holy story
I give God all the praise

The Strength of Joy

When I think of the goodness of Jesus
And all that he has done for me
Something wells up in me that is beyond my emotions
A joy that completely restores
And dries up whatever troubles I thought I was having
A love that soothes better than warm milk on a restless night
A peace that calms my fears, like how a mother consoles her child
    who is afraid of the dark
So many levels to his grace and mercy
To vast and deep to explain in one experience or a million
He is the great I Am
Nobody like Him
Words said by many
Appropriate only until you have experienced him first hand
Ten thousand tongues could not express the gratitude that can be
    enjoyed by all who embrace
We forget so many times when we face obstacles
But He is always there to comfort us
I ask myself
How can I possibly forget after so much goodness?
He reminds me that I am still yet human very flawed and incapable,
I am made strong, in Him
Not by my power and might but God's
God sent His son they call Him Jesus
To be like him is my quest
And to be fulfilled when I meet him is my goals

Confused Importance

Not by my means
To control the uncontrollable
Everyday attempts and misguided ventures
That's life people say
Is this the way it's supposed to be
Does anybody ask that question?
Is the rat race the norm or the perversion?
Many don't know, some forgotten
Questions, truth, blind conformity
What's right, what's wrong?
It's all an illusion, that's mistaken for the truth
The tangible believed to be real and intangible fake
So many levels of reality not seen but in existence
What is important lost in a sea of frivolity
Innocents and compassion
Gives way to insensitive and destructive behavior
Take it back to when locks were rusted in the open position
And doors rarely an obstacle
When full throttle was a speed unheard of
And the fastest thing moving was mom's apple pie
A lie that keeps getting told that bigger and quicker is better
When life is lost for the price
Better get ready they say

Like a voice crying in the wilderness or concrete jungle
You pick, it's the same, more than you know
Nothing new under the sun
Just keeps on getting recycled, same product new cover

God Crazy

Holler it, scream it, and don't be shamed
They do it and brag about it later
How could you not
He has been so good to you
Brought you out of darkness
Into a light so bright it cleaned better than Clorox bleach
You know what I'm talking about
Go crazy lose yourself in it
When the praises go up
The blessings come down
If you knew you could win the lottery just by screaming and hollering
You would do it
Well if you give God the praise
Forget about the lottery
You just might save your mind and everything else your about to lose
You can even win favor with God
That can put you on a runaway train straight to your blessing
So go ahead get your ticket
Give God the praise
This crazy is so sane, this high is so good
When you get there you want believe your eyes
If you don't, don't hinder me
Because I have tasted, and I have seen

But I must warn you
When you go through that door there is no turning back
And it gets better and better
When and if you get there spread the word
This stuff is too good to keep it to yourself
Look I was just like you
But look at me now, just can't help myself
You won't either
HALLELUJAH!!!
I'm not sorry that slipped out
Let me do it again, felt good
HALLELUJAH!!!
God gonna make me get my mind up in here up in, up in here

The Invitation

Do you want to be in the number?
You ought to be in the number
A place where you can exist in time and out
Where the covering of the glory of God
Transcends all evil and trouble
A pocket of space where you are hid
A secret place where even your enemies see you
But can't touch you
An all-inclusive VIP pass that shields you from even death
And ushers you to places where your own intellect or popularity
Good or bad can't take you
To be set apart in an exclusive club
That is not just for the prominent
But for the beggar who is down and out
You don't have to be cut throat, a back stabber, or even a snitch
Being in this group, the one who invited you knows everything
And all of the secrets held by its members
Sounds good yet, it should
Just being you and striving to be Christ like
Is all it takes to stay a member
And guess what, all the goals that you thought you were not smart
    enough to create
The one who invited you is made strong in your weakness and you
    can do it

Let me tell you His name
He goes by several
He is the King of kings and Lord of lords
The Son of man, the Lamb of God
But I have his permission to give you his name given to Him by His
	Heavenly Father
A name above any other
Jesus Christ our Lord and Savior

Precious Gift

Sweet melodies combine and intertwine with humbling expectation
Innocence bathed with beauty
Too precious to be completely shared with words
A compilation of two seasoned with the spirit of love
A growing treasure so priceless Bill Gates could not afford
As the day approaches for your opening to life
Hesitation haunts me on how provision will be satisfied
True for a second I wonder if I am man enough to raise such a prize
Then the vessel of which my pride grows assures me
My rose, my better half, and my help mate
The essence of black beauty that is my Queen
How could a man doubt too long with such a connection
Two staggering gifts that some search for, for a lifetime
My search has been ended, but my drive heightened
To think back to what I thought was important
Buried under present reality
Not words of regret, but thoughts of enlightenment
Could this be real?
Then the evidence of my high praise, assures me it is

The Influence of My Wife

It's like sunshine in the morning, when the day first awakens
New, fresh, and beautiful
You light up my everything
You're like tasty smooth cream
Thick and rich and very tantalizing
The ingredient that goes well with my morning drink
The start that gets me going
She's like a refreshing shower
Cooling me down when I am hot
Warming me up when I am cold
The perfect complement that soothes me to the quick
On the real she is the love of my life that makes me feel alright
My wife, my queen, I have cherished her from the beginning
And I will to the until

A Day

The mist of creation opens and the curtain is drawn
The veil of the night is lifted
Birds chirp and give praise to our God, King, and Heavenly Father
The sun peeks its head above the shoulders of the earth
The symphony of the orchestra begins
Slowly and gracefully the sun climbs higher and higher in the sky
The buzzing of life begins
Sleepy eyes open and hungry tummies quake
Breakfast fills the air with its delicious savor
Adults and children start there day with hard work and play
Energy is expended and time slips by unawares
It's time for lunch and the sun beams down with controlled intensity
Everything is unfolding with the precision of a Swiss clock
I see the sun yawn
It's time for its long trek, back underneath the depths of space
To see another day
To run the same course in the race we call life

The Transfigured Heart

Lord fix my heart that I might fully serve you
Clean up the broken pieces that have collected over time
The hurt that has made me build walls
Where in the stillness, solitude, and silence it leaves me in despair
Please fix my heart, Lord, so that I may show the love you freely give
Help me have the tenderness and compassion
That by your grace can give me peace
I know you are able to, you can do anything
In your magnificent hands, I know my heart is safe
To shape, mold, and create a piece of excellence
And when you are through
Touch me with your merciful hand
For the closeness I desire with you grows ever so strong
Just to be close to you is my request
To grow stronger spiritually
That when I see the hurt and pain,
That was fixed in my heart
In those persons I am sent to help
I can show there is a way out.

Eve of Life

The budding of the fruit which lies inside
That was thought to lay dormant
Begins its first trek into a world that is a mystery, but is well known
    by its inhabitants
The happiness and the very special grows
The perfection that only God can create
Slowly transforming into the complex creature that bubbles over
    with innocence
The final appearance that is full of anticipation
Builds until the climatic end
It's here!! Wow!!
Such beauty, such tenderness, such delicate features
Love can be the only thing that overshadows, what it takes to endure
    this blessed
beginning

Wait!!!

It's so hard to wait
Bills are due, creditors hounding me
God says wait
Seems like more problems arise, I can't keep still
Something, it feels like I gotta due something
God says wait
The walls are about to crumble, and the chasers and catchers are on
    my heels
God says wait
If I try this will I make a mistake?
Oh, Lord, what do I do?
Wait!!!
I say wait!!!
Don't you know I made you and everything around you?
You must learn to be patient and have peace
The world will go on with or without you
Trust in me no matter how it looks
Believe in me not a job or a statement book
For I am the Lord your God
I can give you peace that will keep you in the midst of a hurricane
For I am the eye in the middle and the rock that cannot and will not
    be moved
I don't just want you to wait
I want you to wait and trust me

Open to Your Will

Wherever you want me to go, Lord, I'll go
Whatever you want me to do, Lord, I'll do
Whatever you want me to say, Lord, I'll say
I just want to be in your will
Whatever the storm whatever the test
I'll go through it, just to be closer to you
Send me where no one wants to go
Open doors for me to show, your strength, your power, your grace,
    your mercy
So wherever you want me to go, Lord, I'll go
Whatever you want me to do, Lord, I'll do
Whatever you want me to say, Lord, I'll say
For your words are like music to my ears
Your presence so sweet it comforts me and calms my fears
How precious is your name, Heavenly Father, I love your name
Now I'll listen closely to you
I'll tune my ear to your voice
I'll quiet the noise in my life and I'll search for you with all my heart
So I can go wherever you want me to go, Lord
So I can do whatever you want me to do, Lord
And so I can say whatever you want me to say
I put my trust in you; I put my faith in you
I'll pull my joy from you, because you are my strength, you are my
    hope

I'll never know a better friend than you, so use me to Your Glory
You know when trouble seemed all around
In the night terrors I found that one thing I know for sure, you will
    never leave me all alone
I have been strong in my faith that you will turn my night into day
    and you have
You told me that my storms will come and go, they have, and you're
    still the same through it all
So this I am real sure that I can come out of anything the victor
I am going to stand come what may, I am going to stand every day
I will not back down; I'll keep holding my ground
Until that very day, when you say to me well done
So I'm going where you want me to go, I'm doing what you want me
    to do, and I will say what you want me to say every day

Brand-new Mornings

Thank you for the morning, the peace that surrounds, and the quiet
      that soothes
Feels like love, your love, that comes straight from above
The night seemed so long and the dark so cold
I don't know what I would have done without the morning
It brought sunshine and joy which cleared away sorrow and pain
I'm looking forward to that time when morning will last forever
When night will never fall and rest will be always and forever
I'll take the mornings for now; I will wake up and greet you
So we can talk, and I can listen to your loving voice
I'll go through every night and push on until morning
Just to hear you and to see the beauty of the morning

Praise

Praise God, let everything lift up their voices and praise him
No other one comes close before him
Let heaven and earth exalt his name
Give Him glory that is due
His majesty, His power, His sovereignty, is of the Holiest
He is alpha, omega, beginning, and end
There is nothing He can't do
He has it all to do it all
He reaches the lowest and the highest
What a mighty God we serve
He who created, knows, and sees all things
Let the earth shake with His praise
Let all that is in me give Him the Highest praise
Hallelujah to your most precious and Holy Name
All the credit belongs to him
For their can be no one before or above Him
No greater love have I felt in His presence
No greater joy that can compare
Knowing Him on a level that I thought I could not attain comforts me
He created me and knows me entirely, holds my hand and tells me
    His plan for me
I can't express how great that feels. How happy that makes me
My God talks to me, little insecure me
What a great and merciful God

Love's Fervent Expression

I just want to express my love for you
My deep love for you
To write and sing a beautiful melody
Not for form or fashion, nor fame or glory
Just to put together words so pure and present them back to you
To pour out my joy in rhythmic tones from my spirit to yours
Filling every line with truth, holding back tears and rejoicing
Feeling you since my youth, holding me together
Cradling me with your love, never once leaving me alone
Now showing and entrusting me with your eternal truths
I once thought why me, why so much pain and grief
So visible to me, but invisible to others
I know now that in my weakness you are made strong
And you chose my particular weakness for your strength to show
I thank you for this thorn in my side
If I did not have it I would not have come to know you as I now do
Great is your grace, great is your mercy
You are my God and friend and with you I can win
Nothing is impossible or to hard
You have reshaped my thinking and my perception has changed
Persistent faith unwavering is my claim
Thanks to you my world has changed and I'll never be the same
Hallelujah to Your name

Wisdom in Wrinkles

I look in the mirror, and I see wrinkles where there were smooth lines
Battle scars of living and raising offspring of the next generation
Lines of testament of fulfilled and unfulfilled hopes and dreams
Valleys of smiles and frowns that show the up's and down's of life
Blazed trails that have come and gone
Troubles that are now whispers in the wind
Folds and creases that are a badge of a right of passage that say this
      body has stood the test of time
A body that reflects a lifetime of earned wisdom.
A class of respect and honor
Above all to say the least I am a special part of history
So don't throw me away listen to my story and learn
Your life might not be as hard and uphill as mine
One day all eventually will show wrinkles from a lifetime full of wis-
      dom or regret.

Illness to Victory

They call it a sickness I call it my thorn
To those who don't understand, fear and worry grip them
The aid of medication and counseling are the professionals answer
My answer is Jesus the Christ in whom I am healed
My thorn ever so subtle from my earliest memories
Awakened fully and left me shaken and disturbed
I did not understand what was going on inside my mind and my
    nerves.
It was like I walked in a door that I stumbled upon, but somehow I
    knew was there
After a while my thorn was elevated with prayer and medication
For a while the only thing that kept me was my faith and grip on
    God
Apprehension and doubt was defeated by the Holy Spirit that was
    inside me
That strength gave me courage during tough times
Life seemed to be passing me by during the years of my ordeal
Going from one scene to the next
Even though I was the star of my life it felt like I was the understudy,
    but the story does not end there.
In God's infinite wisdom and power, he led me to my wife that
    brought happiness to my life
I am no longer the understudy of my life

I have reclaimed the starring role with the power and might of my
    Heavenly Father and Lord and Savior Jesus Christ.
I am still kind of shy, but that's just a residual of my thorn, it keeps
    me humble
My message is simply to say that don't let anything hinder you,
    nothing
Look to Jesus He will take you to places and open doors you can't
    perceive or dream of

Greatness of Freedom

That dream that people laid down their life for
A dream where fore fathers crossed the oceans and left behind all that
    was known
A dream where soldiers young and old leave behind families some
    with newborns to fight
Having in the back of their minds this might be the last time they
    see their dear ones
Money, fast cars, houses, etc., seems to be the focus of this dream
Live long enough and go through enough, you will see that's an
    empty course
It is you see the right to live free without bondage, to make your own
    way
Possibly go or send your children to college and become something
A life that is only controlled by healthy limitations, and the ceiling
    of imagination
Yes live long enough to add your sweat, blood, and tears to the cause.
A cost worth living and dying for, the tie that binds all of us in this
    great country
America a country so diverse and full of promise, the drive to come
    here and taste and see is almost irresistible
Just remember the land of the free and the home of the brave is just
    that
The basic element that pushed and pushes courage's hearts to see that
    ever pursuing victory of freedom

Saved

My eyes opened, and for the first time I saw clearly
Grace, mercy, and love abounding in limitless infliction
So much peace and rest in his loving arms
It overwhelms me tenderly
Pride and self-recognition goes out the window, replaced with
humbleness
The very heavy weight of troubles and burdens lifted from my
shoulders
Recognizing a power so great, I knew I was in the presence of God

Refreshed

I've been in my dress shoe mode for too long
Each step is full of dread, you know that feeling
Keeping up appearances for this one and that one
Thinking I can't wait till I get my comfortable on
When hair is let down and belts loosened
When uncomfortable body heat is met with the cold AC
Ah! What a feeling
Like laying back with a tall glass of lemonade or iced tea and not
     having a care in the world
When troubles not only didn't last, but was not present
What a lifestyle, free from the exhausting measures of others, to the
     peace of mind of knowing and loving thy self-faults and all
The true image of life

The Paradise of Innocence

I have tasted of the forbidden fruit
When I was told not to touch, I touched
When I was told not to handle, I handled
When I was told not to look, I looked twice then stared
Now the junk of my past interrupts me every now and then, when I
    am trying to do right
Images and thoughts distracting me while I try to stay focused and
    put my hand to the plow
I know I am forgiven, because the Lord told me in His word
I look back to that state of paradise, when things were easy, clear and
    uninhibited
A time long since passed my memory
No glory is given to the enemy and all praises go to my Heavenly
    Father for he is a keeper
My curiosity now drives me to find the hidden truths of God's Gospel
    a hunger that is unquenchable and inexhaustible
The closer I get to his marvelous light, the lighter my baggage I carry
    gets
Dropping each heavy load and renewing my mind from the useless
    garbage that clouds my thinking
I am the righteousness of God and paradise will be regained once
    more

My Prayer to You

I find myself in your presence telling you all my troubles
Then suddenly I feel a wave of comfort and it fills me with so much joy
I try to contain myself and be quite, but when I think on what you
    have done for me
My heart and body soars with the gratitude of your love
As a man I am in awe how you can hear the cry's and burdens of not
    only me, but the world
As I am humbled by the realization of how great and powerful you are
I am filled with a peace because I know that there is nothing you
    can't handle
Thank you, Father, for being there for me day and night
I know there is none greater than you

On the Road to Destiny

I started on the road today because I heard you mom when you said
    to make your dreams come true
I really wanted to stay and make my own way, but home life was not
    for me
I am on the road again and I admit I started to give in
This passion though won't let me stop, I'll never give up
I know this gift inside me must be shared, so there is no room for
    fear and doubt
I am going to win
The joy inside me when I am functioning in my calling lets me know
    it's from above
Lord, it's been a while and I am older know
I must say you have blessed me so much that the doubters have
    stopped doubting
The fire is still inside, and your message I'll proclaim
I'm giving back what you gave me in service so I can help someone
    that was just like me
It was a hard road to trek, but it was worth it the journey
Stick to your dreams, and as long as you put the Lord first, he will
    show you the right path
And your gift will make room for you

Life After Doubt

How do I run this race, while carrying my cross and walking this walk
Everything seems to be trying to knock me down or trip me up
When I am happy something happens trying to make me sad
When I am upset something tries to push me over the edge
They say it's all a part of life, how soon people forget until it is their
     turn
Why on earth do I get discouraged, I can't help it I am human
I do try to keep a thankful heart and keep my mind stayed on Jesus
Sometimes though you get hit so hard you don't know which way is
     up or down
In short, life stings and can be uncomfortable, we all have been there
     or headed in that direction
So it is imperative to keep living to enjoy those pleasant when we get
     there

Relationship

Touching the very heart of me
Lord only you can see the real me, pass all the masks
Breaking through the facades to get to the core root of me
Being true to you is easy because you see all truth anyway
There is no faking with or tricking you, Lord, and I am glad
The transparency with you gives me peace to my soul, you are my
     peace
Thank you for your understanding and allowing me to have an audi-
     ence with you that surpasses all others, when I need you or just
     want to talk
Every day I love to talk to you sharing my thoughts and gaining your
     wisdom
When I get to you in heaven I know one look will pay for it all, but
     until then
I'll settle for the beauty of what we have now

Progress

Time has unfolded and the baton has been handed off to the next
generation
The transformation of the old world into the new world has taken
place
It was filled with turmoil, fear, and hate, but the resolve of a rainbow
of people kept the hope of a better future alive
Marches, boycotts, and a belief in a God who believes in equality,
pushed a nation to the
place of influence and power, utilizing all of its people
We have faced together internal and external raging wars and growing pains, for reasons that could seem foolish and selfish
Through it all the patience of a people paid off
Victory has been won at the highest level to an intelligent and capa-
ble leader
History will never be the same and a fresh new outlook for this coun-
try has awakened hope again in the young as well as the old
Praise God for change and progress
For when we become stagnant and stale in our beliefs it is the begin-
ning of the end

Victory Unparalleled

This is a fictional story about a young man against all odds stack against him, and he makes it with Jesus Christ. He had to pay his dues of life, but he came out on top. He then gave back to help someone else. This is the story of Robert Lyle. It begins with a loving young couple who find each other during the best season of their lives. The couple courted and ultimately get married. The mother, Susan Wright, was a music teacher who loved to teach and sing on the side. She, one day, was invited to a concert where the famous pianist, Jason Lyle, was to play. Susan, being a lover of music, was swept away by Jason's talent.

After the concert, Susan and her friend went to the party hosted by the musician's agent. Both Jason and Susan were mingling until their eyes met each other's. Jason, being the confident bachelor, approached Susan, which was the beginning of the relationship that led to their marriage. The courtship was beautiful between them.

They took the time to get to know each other and had fun doing it. After two wonderful years of marriage, they had a son named Robert. This blessing was the happiest both parents had been in there lives. Year after year went by, and eventually Robert turned ten. Life could not have been better for the Lyle family. Robert took after his parents of having musical talent and started playing the piano and singing.

Two months into Robert's tenth year of life, tragedy hit. The family was riding in the car when they were hit by a drunk driver. Both Jason and Susan lose their lives, and only Robert survived.

When everything cleared, we find Robert in a coma at the local hospital. In Robert's state, he had a recurring dream of when Susan would tell just before his bedtime that she loved, was proud of him, and that whatever he wanted to do in life, do what it takes to be successful at it. Robert woke up several days later disturbed and confused, asking for his parents. One of the doctors told him kindly the bad news. Robert took the news hard, which made his recovery slow and painful. Every day, Robert was visited by a nice Christian couple who lifts his spirits.

In secret, the couple was visiting Robert because they planned on adopting him. They were friends of his parents and was childless. The day before Robert's discharge, the couple announced their motives to him, and Robert agreed to be there son. The days ahead of Robert was tough, but his new parents led him to Christ, which was very instrumental in the elevating of his pain and anger of what happened to his parents. Robert grew up like any other kid and was an average student in school. Time goes by, and Robert graduated from high school, wondering what he will do with his life. His adoptive father invited him to join him in the family business, which was the running of a restaurant. Robert decided why not and joined the business.

To his surprise, he was very good at the restaurant. A year passed, and we find Robert asleep in his bed, dreaming. He was dreaming the same dream he had when he was in his coma after the wreck that killed his parents. He woke up in a cold sweat, knowing what he had to do.

Robert had been secretly taking lessons to perfect his singing and piano playing. The dream only confirmed what he had been feeling in his heart. In the morning, he told his adoptive father what he was feeling and that he wanted to start his music career in the big city. He was disappointed, but he told Robert to follow his dreams. So Robert heads off to the big city to make his way.

It wasn't as easy as he thought, eventually his money ran out, and he ended up washing dishes at another restaurant in the big city. Too shamed and proud to go back home, he suffered silently. washing dishes to make ends meet. One day, just like any other day,

Robert found himself washing dishes, but he began to sing to pass the time. He is heard by one of the cooks in the kitchen.

The cook thinks to himself that Robert has talent and when his shift was over, he spoke to his brother, a talent agent. The cook introduced Robert to his brother, and he believed the same thing and entered Robert into a talent show. He won. The agent hooked Robert up with a recording deal, and he became an overnight sensation. The years passed, and Robert became one of the best talents in the secular music world. With all the success he had, he fills empty. Yes he has women. throwing themselves at him. and the adoration of his fans, but he remembered his Christian background and how happy he was with much less than he has now.

The next day, he saw a woman that interests him. There was something strange about her though, she knew who he was, but she was not phased at all about him. He had to know more about her, so he found out where she hangs out, and it was the church.

He began to go to church with her and something happened, they became friends. They began a courtship much like his parents did, and then they marry. Robert decided to leave the secular music industry, return to his gospel roots, and become a gospel artist. In his spare time, Robert volunteers his talents to his church and gives music lessons to the children of his church. Eventually, Robert and his wife had two children. a girl and a boy. The story ends with Robert on stage. singing God's praises and him telling his testimony about his life.

This story was meant to encourage someone, that no matter what you go through or start in life, if you end with Jesus, you will have the victory every time.

Presence

The beauty of your presence surrounds me
It engulfs me with the majestic flavor that is uniquely you
To lavish such greatness upon me honors me deeply
It leaves me filled with joy, hope, and a promise of a better tomorrow
My thanks transcends beyond my capability to interpret it vocally
I need, no I must show it with my every being
My walk, my talk, my life, and my praise
To become what your expected calling, for this creation is my pursuit
Weeding through self-doubt and will to blossom into the being that
    was thought of before time started
Your favor I need at all times
Before the parting of my eyes in the morning to the closing of them
    at night
I will not accept none other presence before you
You are the Almighty and Great God.
I lift you up for all to see in my life

Summary of Recommitment

It was not by chance that brought us in Holy Union
Ordained of God, we experience a love that knows no bounds
A life the better because of the two
Connected together until eternity
Let us be reminded this day of the vows we shared
To experience once again the captivation that overtook us that led to
    this wondrous and beautiful journey

Red

So deep and powerful, refusing to let go of stares
Snatching day dreamers and holding a tight grip of passer buyers
Rich and smooth I powerfully fuel the engine of inspiration
Too strong for mildness to bold for weakness
I play for keeps never wasting time for prisoners
I take control of lips and figures, cars sport me as I adorn them
I enhance the makeup of anything
I am the spice for the flavor of life
Red accept no imitations

Purple

I am the very nature of royalty
Kings and Queens seek after my company
I have the flash and my middle name is flare
Soldiers for their bravery carry me on their hearts
Even though time skips by through the centuries I flagrantly tran-
    scend trends
Mistakenly I have been kept from those that could not afford me or
    the ones that were not held in high esteem years ago
Since prejudice has been stomped out and prestige given equally
I am loved and embraced by many
I always and have always held my head up high
Never forgetting who I am
I am purple the color that has only gotten better through the ages

Gold

I have been sought after for untold centuries
The muscle behind dynasties and the foundation of nations
Most who see me must have me and I will not be ignored
My worth and weight speaks for itself
In heat, I am perfected and pressure adds to my character
Athletes of the most elite in the world are graced by my attention for
      their persistent pursuit of greatness
I can be used for great good and beautiful masterpieces, but greedy
      hands smudged my brilliants with the lack of self-control
Nevertheless my resolve shall keep its splendor
Who am I? I am gold proud and strong

I Love You, Alexandria

You were as tiny as a want
You grew into our loving arms and captured our hearts
Glancing as time goes by at your ever blossoming beauty
I am astonished by how your small steps led to jumps and leaps
Already you have a humor that tickles my funny bone and a smile
      that lights up what was a bad day
I could not have known that the treasure that is you could be so pre-
      ciously needed in my life
The future is fortunate and blessed to have in its wait what you will
      become, supplied only by your particular flavor, unlocking the
      mysteries that will crop up in your generation
You are my pride and joy
Love you always, Daddy

About the Author

My name is Danny Sutherland, and I am a native born Washingtonian. I grew up in the foster care system of Washington DC. I am an average guy that also grew up in the Baptist Church. The moment I was born, the odds were stacked against me. My mother gave birth to me by herself in a one bedroom apartment. I almost died from suffocation when I was two. By the time I was three, I was in the foster care program. Life was not easy because I suffered from personal adversities, which caused me to be different from my peers. For a long time, I did not know what was wrong with me. Thinking clearly was an obstacle for me. Sometimes, I could not hold my head up because of self-esteem issues. The one thing that kept me through it all was my faith in God. I eventually was counseled properly, and now I am married to a beautiful woman and blessed with a daughter. This book is a reflection of my thoughts and feelings to encourage someone that even though life may not be easy, if you trust in the Lord, you can make it.

www.ingramcontent.com/pod-product-compliance
Lightning Source LLC
Chambersburg PA
CBHW031330290526
45784CB00014B/2511